BLUE
with
BLOOD
in it

a
Blue
with
Blood
in it

elizabeth   *philips*

COTEAU BOOKS
TWENTY-FIVE YEARS

Edited by Don McKay.

Cover photo by Andrew Leyerle.
Cover and Book Design by Duncan Campbell.

Printed and bound in Canada at Houghton-Boston Lithographers, Saskatoon.

Canadian Cataloguing in Publication Data

Philips, Elizabeth

A blue with blood in it

Poems.
ISBN 1-55050-174-7

I. Title.

PS8581.H545 B58 2000   C811'.54   C00-920159-9
PR9199.3.P458 B58 2000

COTEAU BOOKS   AVAILABLE IN THE US FROM
401-2206 Dewdney Ave.   General Distribution Services
Regina, Saskatchewan   4500 Witmer Industrial Estates
Canada   S4R 1H3   Niagara Falls, NY, 14305-1386

The publisher gratefully acknowledges the financial assistance of the Saskatchewan Arts Board, the Canada Council for the Arts, the Government of Canada through the Book Publishing Industry Development Program (BPIDP), and the City of Regina Arts Commission, for its publishing program.

"When the twisted tree shall become my body
Then I shall begin to live out my natural span."

— MENG CHIAO

CONTENTS

part one: The Clearing

Wild Blueberries — 3
Fruitfulness — 4
The Night Before — 5
Wings — 6
All Day — 8
Low Tide — 9
Ice Time — 13
November: Far Past — 14
Beginning — 16
A Woman Walking — 18
The Clearing — 20

part two: The Heart as a Way

Reply To The Minister Of Lilies — 25
Yellow — 27
Witness — 28
Violet — 32
Gardener Of Snow — 33
Wild Mint — 35
Learning To Skin — 36
Perfect Skin — 37
Orange — 38
Red — 39
New Leaves — 41
Blue — 42
What You Are About — 44
History Of Red — 45
Owl's Clover — 46
The Heart As A Way — 49

part three: The Garden, Remembered

Parable Of New Wood — 53
D-Day — 55
Yes — 57
In This Country — 58
The Hypnotist's Wife — 61
Sleepwalking — 63
The Garden, Remembered — 66

part one

the
CLEARING

Wild Blueberries

After hours on the shallow northern lake, green
then silver, then green, we drift into the far shore, a brief
crescent of beach behind reeds, hiss of sand
as the keel runs aground. We lift the boat from the water, hand
over hand. At the edge of the beach, fringed
gentians. Their blue
not teal, not sapphire, not sky. A blue
with blood in it.

We walk up through juniper
into a meadow flocked with low-growing blueberries.
They ring our ankles like amulets
on sprung stems. We step back
onto a bed of moss, glance at each other:
                                                    bear. She must
be there, farther back, watching.
Sun wedges through spruce, hot, monolithic.
We feed each other handfuls, taste of light
tempered by conifer, our teeth sprayed blue.
In the background, indigo
shadows, live, wind-whipped darkness, stippled
like fur. We kiss, slow but wary, eyes open.

Time to go. We want more
but we feel her, the breath
                            of her waiting.
We walk back down through juniper to gentian, launch the boat,
our smudged mouths knowing, for the moment, what the bear
knows. Blue of late summer, blue of northern duff,
a meadow of peeled light, and beyond, the entrance
to caves of spruce, birch, aspen, the bent trunks of wind.

Fruitfulness

The day is bright, the wind heavy like drenched silk
after weeks of rain. She sits at an open window, stares out
at the sun-shattered sea. Something in the air reminds her
of saskatoons, their seedy tartness. How her mouth
went purple with them, afternoons when she was a girl
in Saskatchewan, eating pie and ice cream in her grandmother's kitchen.

He is in another part of the house, his mind travelling
in sly electronic signals across the city. He is plotting
the resurrection of the dragon, the newly configured
pathways of its brain. A leathery young reptile, it wants
to know how small a blossom the soul is, to fly
to the edge of extinction and back.

She gets up from her desk and wanders into the kitchen, still tasting
saskatoons. She sees a scene in a movie, a five-year-old girl
in a garden, hugging a white gallon pail, eating with precise
fingers, one small hand inked
violet, the other clean and white. When the girl looks up, distracted
by a bee in the cornflowers, the whole blue prairie
sky rises out of her eyes.

He leaves his screen and joins her in the kitchen.
"I have a dragon by the tail," he says, filling a glass with cold water.
"Oh," she says, shaking her head a little, as if seeing him
for the first time, "What colour?"
"It's purple," he says, taking a sip, "the colour of..."
"...of saskatoons," she guesses. "Yes, but it's a sea-
dragon," he says, "with huge hollow feet like pontoons."

They go to the window, where the Pacific is dark
with downed light, waves sharp and overlapping like scales.
The sea is home now. The tide pulls
at the bottom of their dreams. Home, but its primeval distances
remember for them that other place, where the sun swims
in buffalo grass and the stain of berries
won't wash away.

The Night Before

The night before the diagnosis
is confirmed, we drink red wine, a French
Syrah, one bottle before, another following
the pasta and bread, the salad of butter lettuce.
We eat carefully, the forks and the knives
barely scraping the plates.

John tells a story about harvest
and how he ran between farmhouse and
threshing crew, bearing pails of water toward
their thirst, and then
away, the empty pails sailing in his easy
grip, the new strength in his lengthening
stride making him almost
clumsy.

Outside, the white lights strung in the Russian Olive
are a beaded curtain between
the shadows at our wrists when we lift
our glasses, and the darkness
beyond the tree, the diminishing
cold and snow of late spring.

We ask for another story
and Gail tells of meeting John
for the first time, thirty years ago in a rose garden
overlooking Toronto, both of them longing
for the North, for Shield country and the living

stone underfoot. And this
is how the evening passes, in fresh
water, in grapes, in the recounting of first
understandings. And in laughter
soft in the mouth, no trace of acid
not even in the pauses between words,
or after.

Wings

She who was once unfaltering — her reading voice like butter
with lemon — looks up, drops
a syllable, looks down. She is watching a fly
crawl across the back of her hand; it spirals away
over the people who murmur around her. But it's not the people
who are stirring — they are still and listening
as she turns the page — it is the words that are moving like bees
through the honeycomb. What was she

saying about this poem, written
so long ago? There are honeybees, and the man
who keeps them. He waves a smoking wand, an otherworldly
priest. Funny, she thinks, how insects have always
attracted her, carried her off
on transparent wings, their feet sticky as a thought

that will not let her go. Even young
and ripe and on the verge
of perfect pleasure, she was diverted by a fly
scaling the green and gold leaves of the wallpaper,
Paris, 1938. The fly, she thought, *musca domestica,*
the same on either side of the Channel. A laugh
rises in her, despite the attentions of the Frenchman
so cunningly at work between her legs, his tongue
a wet strawberry. He gave

her two weeks of rainy afternoons in his room
above Rue Belanger. Her first lover, the touch of his
wiry cabinetmaker's hands and the hair on her arms
shivered. Her French was fine, she thought, yet she never
seemed to understand, except when he spoke
with fingertips, with the articulate lines

of his palms. She closes the book. The audience
will not have noticed how she became, for a second,
the bluebottle, circling and indifferent over their inert
human shapes. The bee poem was good.
What was the beekeeper's
name? Those coffee-coloured eyes

look up at her, his chin on her belly, and the fly
on the wallpaper. How strange, she thinks, stepping down
from the stage, to have been dead these sixty years,
killed early in the war. She feels a kick
in the pulse in her wrist, like the small spasm
he made inside her, not at all what she'd expected.
The thick spray cooling on her inner thigh, on the blue sheets.
Outside, the faint hum of Paris, 1938, as she leans back
amid applause.

In memoriam

All Day

The only sun all day is a single fleeting shaft that touches,
briefly, the backs of his hands as he works, cutting deadwood
beneath the pines. He glances up

to the peaks of the tall trees as a bright swath of mist
sails over, running lower and faster
than the ceiling of high cloud. Earlier that morning

he gathered young mushrooms in the meadow, silky
buttons, their gills still enshrouded
in snowy skin, choosing

several of the freshest, placing them under a towel
in his basket. Now he stretches his arms above his head,
letting the long axe-handle tip over

onto the pine duff. Later, he'll rinse the mushrooms
in the stream, then eat them with the eggs
his wife packed last night.

He bends over and picks up the axe. It will be many years
before he learns that when the mushroom's pale sheath
tears, leaving a ridge around the stem, you call it

the ring, and while the skin is whole and untorn,
the universal veil. When his grandson reads this to him
from a book on wild mushrooms,

he'll shake his head, as if he'd never known
how to tell the choice from the poisonous. He'll see the child's
smooth face and remember the day

sun blessed his hands, once, before the clouds closed again,
and gripping the polished handle
he went back to work.

Low Tide

i

I learned to swim, your grandfather says
as you crouch beside his blanket
on the fine bleached sand.

*I crossed the river
without feet,* he says.

You shrug, liking the sound of that
but know he can't swim, not with those gnarled
arthritic paws.

You pass him tea in a thermos, then leap up
and race away, shrieking, into the sea.

ii

You slip into the quiet of the surf, a hush
that's a kind of noise, like what whales
must hear. You duck under, hang there
hugging yourself, counting, *one two
three four.*

No feet, you think, trying to stand
on your hands, breath leaking
from the corner of your mouth,
eight nine ten.

iii

He wishes you had stayed, listening
at his side.

Sand, water,
ice, he thinks, following you
as you lunge headfirst, embracing
a wave.

He shudders
as the sea takes you.

iv

The water is deliciously
cold. You forget everything but the salt
waves and a floating like
flight. In the shallows, stagger
up, quills of water spilling
from outstretched arms.

v

He's not surprised how easily you swim.
Once he was as sure, ran
when walking would do. One morning
he ran away from everything he'd known. Or so
he thought then. He sees himself running
toward the valley where your grandmother
made grain into flour, flour into bread.
Day after day he walked and ran and walked
over rain-washed stone and wet forest floor,
his boots always soaked. The bones of his ruined
feet, arrows in a quiver of skin.

vi

The wind flares and he can't see anything
but sand, or is it the white of the last
dawn before the valley found him, half-starved,
carrying his boots in one hand?

That old journey unwinds
in his head. He skips backwards over stone
and peat and fallen trees, feet young
and straight, until he's at the gate
again, entering the Minister's garden.

vii

You are shouting at him now, you want him
to watch you stand on your hands
underwater, balancing
the sky on the soles of your feet.
But he can't hear you, the noise of the surf
is the sound his hoe makes, biting
into the ground, hacking out the roots
of spent pea vines.

viii

Once you were light, so light he carried you
ten years, a blur in one eye,
until your mother was born. The first time

he held his daughter he knew
you
were inside *her* now, the petal
within the petal.

ix

He throws his weight into the blade and the dry
soil cracks, throwing dust
in his eyes. Hands over his face, he sees
a small girl, spectral
in the sea-light, swimming upside down,
smooth feet like fronds
shooting out of the sea.

Ice Time

On a day as cold as it's ever been, I think of you
thirty years ago in the Arctic, walking the hills
in sealskin boots. The instant before you go down
I see the world as it was for you, a blue haze of
Arctic spring, the horizon
thawing into a mirage of open sea, a breeze catching
at your sleeves. But then your foot slips, heel hitting
slush, water under old snow flows like oil,

                             and you plunge
fifty, one hundred metres towards the blank
edge of the world.

You fell, you say, because you failed to understand
where you were, as if those hills, engraved
glass of the north, were an immaculate garden
where a woman might make an easy hike to the summit
and gaze out through the lens of spring
light, finding a clear passage to summer.
As if all she needed were the courage to look down
from that height, and she'd know for the first time
where she was going.

Only luck stopped you, a callus of snow
in just the right place. And each time I want to reach out
and calm you, my hand inside your sweater, over your
shuddering heart. But I know you will always be alone
when you fall.
               I look out at this day, cold
as it's ever been, and colder, the wind a crystalline
whip, and I see you blinded on the face of the hill –
it's always the moment before you drop,
and my arm, instinctive
as a mother's,
             flies out
and never
in time.

November: Far Past

The three women press close, looking at family
pictures. Fall light, the colour of old paper, in squares
on the table. The mother
speaks in riddles. *Oh,* she says,
bending to the floor, *I've dropped my cloud,*
and they all see it, the white handkerchief on green
tile, cumulus above the fields.

The two daughters watch her eyes, her sudden
smile. They turn for her, carefully, the dry
leaves of the album. Her words
drop one by one into the quiet there, at the table,
well-polished stones resisting memory's
turbulence. *Milk, winter wheat, time to plant
potatoes, the girls and Dad gone to church,
the barley poor again, this much butter
and three eggs.*

They listen as their mother riffles through
the far past, wringing and wringing her hands.
The people in the photographs waver
under their new names, as if they could be
anyone, their lives a litany of possible
phrasings.

Seventy years ago she finds herself posing
beside a stone well, still
not quite a woman. Her hands, strong and work-scarred,
cover the page. She seems to sink down into it —
crosses the farmyard carrying a pail. *Woodpile, fence,
stoneboat, the kettle, the cold
cold water.*

To her daughters their mother's voice
is the ringing inside a well. They call to her, pull
and pull on the rope, drawing her back
out, into the ordinary day. She shows them her cupped
hands, but there's nothing in them
except light. She folds and folds it,
saying, *It rained then, it rained
and rained, yes*

it did rain.

Beginning

I remember cold sand, my soles hardened
from running over gravel, arms buffed smooth
after months of playing on the wind-

polished beach. I sit, chilled, knees to chest,
feet burrowed in sand. I am the only one
left, the shore littered with footprints, churned up

by the last of the summer crowds. But this
is foreground, the up-close. Where I am
is out over water, the spangled fish-

smelling water, a whole horizon of it.
The sky clots and thickens, and I
grow colder, flow away from my skull's

noise, going into the littoral
rhythm, out and away
from the lakeshore, soaring as far

as I can dream going, beyond the harbour and
the fishing boats and the last spit of land, to hang
between water and moving sheets of damp September air.

I swing there, clean and rinsed,
a pebble in the lake-mouth,
but flying hard

into the grey on grey of mist,
as far as the rolling whitecaps, way
out, losing the ground, groundedness,

weight. I recall the trajectory, the flight, the point
where there is nothing
but water below and above, and the storm

that follows, when I don't know
what's moving – the sky, the lake, or my spinning
child self. That was the beginning,

as I remember it. Then I got up,
wandered home for supper, the first
drops of a long rain darkening

my shoulders. In my pocket, a thin
riddled stone, light
as a wish.

A Woman Walking

                    is a pendulum
her momentum   swaying from one
hip   to the other   and back
again   the real and the possible in perfect
flux   if ever she walked out

under a different set of stars   the laws of physics
suspended   if ever she walked through
ether   her bones medieval
and mysterious
                         then she could walk forever
fuelled only by the apple
snagged on her way out
of the garden.

With a baby on her shoulder and a year-old
kid on her back
                         she might keep on going
she might circum-
                         navigate the globe   if ever
she escaped her usual
round

                    and if the man
hadn't stopped her
mid stride   to ask the time
and then   stepped out with her
the load of firewood balanced on her head
                              just the kind of hat
he admired on a woman
                              of course now
she must walk half-

cocked   one foot off
the path where it narrows
she must admire his handsome
walking stick   with its carved knob
shaped like a lion   this third
leg   she thinks
shall give rise to terrible inventions   to *hike*
she hears him say   to *march*
disturbing   her perpetually
elegant gait   defining it by destination
by distance   making her head
hurt.

The Clearing

The woman does what her husband has forbidden and hauls
　　　pail after pail of water up from the creek. She's preparing
　　　　　to clean, one last time before the birth, the two rooms

of their house. She's careful, carrying the weight
　　　with both arms, reaching for sure footing on the wet
　　　　　bank, making herself stop

beside the first of the last asters to bloom, their feathered
　　　whiteness in the grass. She scrubs the year's grime
　　　　　from the walls, the soft scarred floors.

When the water goes grey, she dumps it on the garden
　　　and walks to the creek for more. She works for hours
　　　　　lost in the rhythm,

recalling their first weeks, how afraid she was
　　　alone all day while he cut wood.
　　　　　But now

the child is quick within her.
　　　She rests often, sits at the window, this labour
　　　　　nothing against what it took to claim the land

from spruce, the path worn between garden
　　　and house, the long narrow plot broken
　　　　　from rock, and most of the summer's

vegetables in jars in the cellar. When she's almost
　　　done, the air in the house raw from the harsh soap,
　　　　　she sees the bear

grazing on berries at the far side of the clearing.
      He eats slowly, a kind of tenderness in how he takes
          the fruit from the branch, his cinnamon fur

shimmering with sun. She remembers
      cinnamon, wonders if it is anything but a colour
          in this country. She opens the door

just to show herself, and the bear's head
      swings toward her. Standing on the threshold, she's above
          the animal, and his looking

cannot harm her. His eyes
      glitter with a contained dark, like the two wells in her old
          village, full of stony distances.

There, the bears are all in stories, they rear up
      on two legs like men, roaring
          for blood. She begins to tell the child a story

about how the bear came
      to eat her loneliness, the scent of her mother's
          sweat carried to him on the late

summer air. The bear turns back
      to the berries, the few left too small and dry
          for jam. The woman can't see

how the story will end. The bear may return
      each year to strip the bushes, savouring what grows
          in this meadow that is not

a meadow. Or he comes only as a lithe
        shadow at dusk. By morning the cold breath of mist
            will have fallen and sweetened the berries,

the fruit telling her each time she swallows it
        of the mouth she left in that other place, her thirst
            bending over first one well,

then the other, seeking in the blindness of that stone
        the truth of the water
                she was born to.

part two

the
HEART
as a
WAY

Reply To The Minister Of Lilies

The garden you recall has changed little, only the trees
are taller. Weeds grow like spears of rain
upturned, seeking heaven. This morning I heaped the wheelbarrow
with used-up poppies, sour grasses. The greatest portion
of my labour is spent pampering corn and squash and sweet melons
for the soldiers. Yet my heart remains with the ornamental
plum, the flowers I am allowed along the borders.
Your letter arrived just in time.

I needed your reminder of the first lesson, which is to go
slow, even when I hear the Emperor's assistant, his horse's hooves
ringing in the courtyard, as he dismounts
before the weekly inspection. Even when the vines increase
by the hour, green twine snaking closer and closer
to our Northern sun. How often you said a gardener must move
carefully among the beds, because although the gods
are negligent, they are often watching, and the greatest offence
is the thoughtlessness of haste.

I remember the day you left, we drank green tea in the new
excavation, a pit I would later transform into a pond
for the Emperor's koi. We sat on earth shelves, our feet in clay,
shoulders against black soil going grey in the dry heat, blue
cups steaming in our palms.

I open your letter while standing on the flat stones we chose
earlier that summer, dug from a farmer's field. I ran ahead
of the cart — more athletic than your other students — while you
held the mule. I stacked the stones along the path
as if already placing them in the garden, so eager was I
to please you.

I am, like the garden, much the same. I will do all you ask
and more. I have often dreamt of travelling south to find you
in your exiled garden. I imagine you there now, five hundred miles
and a saltwater bay between us. Your cloth coat is the same blue
as the larkspur growing wild by the village well. In the dream,
you always keep your back to me, a discipline
I have only just begun to understand. I can be sure it's you
only by the sweet smell of your special tobacco.

I put the letter in my pocket, ink smeared by water
from the rain barrel, and return to the rose, the new graft
I was digging in when the messenger came. I widen the hole
and then flood it, pail by pail. The dark water coils like blood
in the heart. My hand is steady, although my breath
trembles like the single stalk of the young rose. I have learned
to give nothing away.

As the years pass, my hands become more and more
your hands, the fingers angular and strong, the seams of skin
engraved with earth. These are the lines that have connected us
even when there was no news, and I had to be content
to search for your words among the lilies and the weeds.

The rose is planted. I pick up the hoe and move
to the flowering beans. I feel the letter in my pocket, its slight
weight, as I slice through roots of bull thistle and goats-
beard, and begin to compose the reply I will send with the boy
who waits, drinking lemon water in the shade of the apple tree
you planted decades before I was born. *I will come as soon
as the melons are ripe on the vine. It will take many months,
but I know that because you have asked it, the journey
will seem small, like the time between rain
and the smell of rain.*

Yellow

He is surrounded by marigolds, small gold coins
as big as his one-year-old fist. He sways, falling
over their scent, hummocks of acrid air that slow him
down, make him see the sun up close. He stares
at the flowers, bending to their heat, practises
his new grasp, plucking the soft petals.

His belly wants its share, as it always does,
and he stuffs them one by one
into his mouth, until he can taste
that colour, the mildest
lemon, and then spits them out
laughing, red lips
in flower.

All through his life he dreams of gold petals —
they blossom in his hands, his arms, and when
he's finally a man, from between his legs, a strangeness
he can't quite get over.

He's dozing away the morning when he has the last
dream, a blooming in his palms, and he wakes
smiling, tries to tell the nurses he's been in bed so long
he's become the place where spring
turns to summer, but the words tangle, his tongue
rooted in his throat.

This morning, he who has smelled nothing for the last year
inhales the sharpness of marigolds, each breath measured
by a century of prairie summers, too many days
to remember. And yet he does, and each slow hour is *yellow,*
yellow, yellow.

Witness

A garden is not what you think, not sweet peas,
not filtered light, not a room sketched out of trellised
roses, clay pots, terraces, but a red
flower and its grey
shadow, what is chosen, what is begotten
and sown, nourished and pruned,
what is thrown on the fire, what is blasted and scythed
and stripped away.

*

Today, the ratter fell on a rat in the compost, one jagged
pounce and shake, his whole body
in the air, breaking
the enemy, an intolerable
scuttling sheathed in matte fur.

The gardener dropped
her hoe, startled by this lightning
out of blue sky, elemental strike against
her weeding calm, like a seizure
of mind, her head scoured
for an instant, emptied of
                              everything,
her heart lunging, wild
for the chase.

*

Two bees spill out of a half-closed rose,
mid-air orgy of greed, buzzing
argument.

The pink flower, released, quavers
on its stem. She
pulls more weeds, unwanted

green cast aside, clasp
and unclasp of thin gloves, stained
knees, the rhythm of
digging in close, sweat,
bruised weeds, standing back,
roses.

*

The stillness of the garden, slow work
of piety and heaped praise,
an illusion, broken
as the lily, scarred
red star
opens,
a thread of yellow on each
petal, flawed
song, wet stamens already
souring.

*

By afternoon the bees are among the poppies,
tumbling the yellow paper cups, and the gardener
works through this tumult of sexual
longing, smeared with it, buttery
streaks of pollen, clinging odour of blood
meal, sodden peat and humus,
the smouldering, the extinguished
fires.

*

Newly arranged
beds, creamy
violas and the preternatural
blue of lobelia.
                    She shunts seedlings
from one bed to another, the shade
garden, the herbaceous
border, the everlasting
search for truth
in composition.
                    Her sullen
willfulness as she overturns the natural
order, metal
of desire, her spade, her trowel
slicing into the friable, the carefully
amended soil.

*

She learns to speak it by putting earth in her mouth,
taste of bone meal and mint.

By hauling compost, whacking out fescue,
quack grass, she learns

to speak it, by accident, a small
bee mistakes her mouth for a red petal (stung gums).

By thorn and nettle, by fork
and tine, she learns to speak it.

By high summer has grown
almost fluent in its language, swollen

pod, shrivelled
stem, memory of clematis, wild

hop vine. By fall
she is all grammar.

She tends to leaf mould and thatch,
scorched by rasping prairie heat, wind

a dry husk, seed
on the tongue.

*

She vows
to see heaven
now, for she has planted meconopsis, the holy
blue poppy that is not a poppy, but
the image of the sky just at
dusk, satin cut
from the wholeness of day, the amen
she says she is owed
before evening, before another
night of raked stars, slinky green
aurora, before
she dies.

Violet

These are the days of gathering in, when air chafes
against itself, heavy with unshed rain, wind
tearing shocked leaves. The garden is worn
yet riotous, the many hues stained, spilling over
one another. Only the tall asters are fresh,
tough blue heads shining on the extreme
edge of summer. Each night the upper air sinks
down, closer and closer to the point where rain
shatters into sleet, and sleet
blossoms into snow.

It is that conjugation she wants to meet, eyes
open. To see blue water
become violet ice, summer blanched
and held. She waits for the thousands of petals
to be cut and milled
by frost, ground into pure
absence.

Waiting, she gathers yellow and bitter
orange, blue and Persian red, and her mouth
waters. When, late one afternoon, snow blows in
from the north, it sweeps across her face
like the annunciation of silence,
the silence of the stilled root, in which dreams
are coloured, spring by spring.

Gardener Of Snow

Winter's first daylong fall, a
squall out of nowhere, finds her
snow-blind but still gardening.
She struggles to recall last
plantings, where she buried
new tulips, those small papery
apples, delicious fruit of next
year's bearing. She worked bulbs in
wherever she found room, and later,
after the ground froze, spread a mulch
of dry leaves, their smell
like tobacco, ritual
cosseting. And now she covers
the same vulnerable sleepers
with snow. Godsend
snow, starfield of seeds, profligate
grains that grow nothing but more
cold.
     November in Saskatchewan
means she must shift bushels of snow
onto the green and red and yellow
and magenta of aster, lilium,
sedum, delphinium, hemero-
callis, aconitum.
              After this she's free
to go inside and forget the many names
the world has given chlorophyll
until the days of unimaginable

April — that moment when sun calls
heat and the helpless earth answers
spring, when the slowly warming
humus grows wonderfully
articulate and sings
in green tongues:
                    phloem,
pitch,
balm,
resin
and sap.

Wild Mint

And then a door opens at the end of a tunnel of leaf-heavy
trees and you're back on the path
through aspen, the understory
glistening beneath the lenses of yesterday's rain
and you find false dragonhead, self-heal and giant
hyssop, one after the other. And they're all mint
when it comes down to it, as if the world's decided
on freshness over

decay, everything radiating an uncluttered, clean
fragrance, and for the moment you've recovered your old
clarity, eyes keen and blossoming over each

green quill, each arrow

separate yet tangled in the grasses, all the lavender
flowerheads, tangled, knotted, frayed and
pointing at you. *But*

was there a door? You whirl to face the trail curving away behind you.
No door. Just a quickening, an
astringency, the place
you slough off the grey of habitual

inattention. This is where the mint came in, the thinnest knife-
blade peeling back the layers to reveal the thirst
inside each stem, stems like straws
siphoning the alkali goodness of soaked

clay, and everywhere you look, careening from green
to green, the world exhales

mint, entreating you
to taste it.

Learning To Skin

Learning to skin green chiles, a thin and potent smoke
rises from the pan, to pin the jalapenos
with a spatula, feel the skins pop as they blister
and char, to flip their blackened pods into a paper
bag and leave them steaming
in their own heat. Learning this new trick, I draw a line

around the hour, separate it from the blur of other
days, just as a poem or song does, anything composed
of a particular longing. The smoke tastes red
and dangerous. I open the door
to let it escape and winter air flares
like a ghost. I love

the language of bodies: veins, flesh, glands,
these are the parts of a chile. I slit open
the jalapenos, cut out the seeds
and what they cling to, petal of spongy
tissue. Even the placenta
is a simple shock of green
on a day when wind lashes white streets.

I peel away the burnt skin, dice them for salsa
and we eat, the sweat on our brows sweet
and vernal. Hours later, settling into sleep, my
lips brush my fingers and taste that wild
oil, faint simmering on the tongue the last of a desire
to make this winter lie down
and die, our mouths awake
and singing.

Perfect Skin

Truly, she doesn't think she'll ever eat wild mushrooms. Not after the large cap she placed on the sideboard – its pinkish bloom like an ad for perfect skin – seemed to melt overnight, and underneath its collapsed parasol, a mass of white worms.

Maggots, she knew, though she'd never seen them before, a writhing so terrible it brought into focus everything she'd been hoping not to encounter in her own home: the voracious inner life, her own creeping subconscious newborn and ravenous in the heart of her clean white kitchen.

Orange

I want the orange
you are eating. I know
I could have had my own, you offered

one from the bowl, but I want
yours, and laughing, you feed
it to me, section by section, until

my mouth is full, the pursed
sweetness opens
and I swallow it. The orange

is as fine as I thought
it might be, acid bound to sugar in a skin of
barely skin, the pleasure not just

in the fruit, but in the taste of your finger-
tips, the bitterness
of where you've been. Where

have you been? In the garden
gathering marigolds, Persian
zinnias, that's where I

would have you, but the goodness
is also in what is not quite
delectable, dry summer heat, the peel

shuttered in your palm, my bare
shoulders, and all
I cannot consume, sorrel

distances, your eyes
on mine, and then the shift,
the looking away.

Red

When summer finally comes, it is a summer like no other in the history of that place. All spring a cool rain falls, and when late in the day the sky lightens, fog clings in drifts over the fields. The children run out to play, and each time they begin their story in a different place, by the sea, or on the side of a mountain. Until the day the sun rises and a searing heat settles over the new wheat. In the pasture, last winter's frost-heaved stones lie steaming on the ground like fresh loaves. The days that follow are too hot for work or play, only the essential chores are attended to, and afterwards, everyone sits in the shade of the oaks, drinking ice water, marvelling at this strange season.

Every Sunday it rains, beginning just before dawn and ending as the worshippers stand gossiping on the church steps after the service. The lady's slippers lining the path on the way home, once a rarity, bloom in their thousands, yellow slippers with thick red laces. The men, used to worrying about a lack of rain and the threat of early frost, gather evenings on the verandah, telling stories no one has heard before. The one about the fish in the rain barrel, and the baby born with all its teeth, and nails long and hooked like claws. The men fold their hands over their bellies, never once speaking of the corn, filling early and sweet, or the wheat, grown taller than even the grandmothers can remember.

The women tell stories too, but in secret, when two or three happen to go down into the cellar at the same time, for potatoes, or just for the cool air, or when they're kneeling together, weeding between rows. They speculate about the future, as if anything can happen now – after this. The leaves of the hop vine are as large as a man's head, they say, imagining the richness of the beer, that the men will want to dance at the harvest festival, as they did when they were young, far into the night.

But it is the roses that are the greatest wonder in this year of abundance. The women grow more and more distracted by the perfume that reaches even to the open windows of the summer kitchen. In the rose garden itself, the air is so suffused it's almost pink, and more than one woman has fainted there, lying undiscovered in the tall grass until the sun sets and she wakes, her skin damp and sweet. Try as they might to stay away, each finds herself alone in the stillness of the afternoon, gazing up into the thicket of vines. It is as if she seeks the answer to a question she's never before thought to ask. And yet when she arrives beneath the trellis, all that matters is the meaning of the colour red, so engorged by sun are the roses: such fullness, a heart might close, petal after petal, and once closed, refuse, ever again, to open.

New Leaves

The garden is threaded with the staccato flight of white-
throated sparrows, from tree to pond to fence
and back again, each takes a turn bathing in the green
cup of water hyacinth. They do not long
for the sun. Perhaps the yellow smudges in front of their eyes
lend their vision the warmth I must reach for
with my hands.

But the morning when the sun returns after ten days of rain
I find their singing in the early hours
has greater weight, though also
lightness, almost sculptural, some impromptu
architecture of dawn. It rises

like a tree
drawn out of several pure notes, thin bark stretched tight
over the many gold branches. But it is the new leaves
at the crown that matter. Their filigree
holds the singing aloft, thousands of small silences
pushing against sun. The shivering young leaves

separate the air that is wind
from the air that is music.

Blue

I walk out at sunrise, early light throwing blue
shadows over knee-deep snow, the air
cold, fragrant with smoke

from the house stove. A horse trail leads
into the bush, my boots huge
beside the stitches a shrew has made

circling the high drifts, whimsical
fringe along the cutline. As I walk
the light grows tinged with sulfur, though blue

lingers under the tall spruce. Far off,
a woodpecker drills in deadwood. A raven
flaps overhead, her call

a swallowed bell. In the old swamp, dry reeds,
struck by wind's vibrato, have etched lines
in the snow, a calligraphy

subtle as the first brush of age
around the eyes. The last storm's heavy fall
has loaded down the scrub, wands of high-bush

cranberry bent into ribs, fresh arcs of snow
lashing everything into place
for the long moment that is winter.

A lightning-felled spruce, its cracked trunk
held up by neighbouring branches, shrouds
the path. Here, the light is blue

on blue. A mist along the ground, it fades away
when I dip my hands in it,
a bloom of colour so ephemeral

it can't be gathered in, but must be known
aslant, like time
or love.

What You Are About

What you are about
to do, kneeling. One hand
brushing a hair from your mouth.
What you are about to do, I
have been waiting for, a weight
in my belly, all
day.
       I lie back, for what you
are about to do. A candle flickers
in the window. Your gaze drops and I feel
your eyes on what you are about
to enter into, your eyes
closing. Whatever it is, what you are
is what I, my fingers
grasping at the sheets, is what I
am.
       All day, a candle, my hands
flickering. What you are about to do now
is what my gaze
wants. To close. To close
on you, the weight
lifting.

History of Red

I want to revisit the red earth, thermal
vents under the sea where some say
life began. Where the sea floor makes
and remakes itself, rising and falling
like the waves miles above, only
much slower. Think of it! A slit in the throat
of the world, heat, water, a few spare
elements, and that rogue,
desire, an aquifer rushing beneath
theory, the squared root of wonder.
But how can anything begin? Can you remember
not being here — they say each of us began in a uterine
sleeve and then slipped down into the crimson
cup. On a day like this, when July consumes
the city and all leaves swell in the compress
of air, it is almost possible to believe this is also
the red earth — if I look long enough at the ash tree,
sinuous with heat, I believe I will know
the answer. And it will not be
any number. It will not be *yes*
or *no*.

Owl's Clover

Late summer in the Qu'Appelle, the russet and fawn-
coloured hills shimmer with finished
grasses, wind glancing off brittle seed heads, tensile stems.
Underfoot, grey light stirs, sage like smoke
in flower. I am not quite awake as I begin
to climb, heat haze already rising, summer
about to turn.

*

I follow deer trail and fox trail, eyes down, searching
for new names for this heat, *dotted blazing-
star, silverleaf psoralea, locoweed.* I have learned
one flower after another, the season a slow
bouquet of stalks, panicles, leaves, the details
of arrangement. And each day I hope to trust
in more than one colour at a time, more than one
leaf, but what comes first is the luminous, the
individual, what separates
aster from aster, sagebrush
from sage.

*

After a summer of walking here, I am almost through
with differences. From the highest hill, I track
the descent of four coulees. I half close
my eyes, trying to see the broad strokes, the path
of grasses chasing the hillsides, twisted
green scrub in the draws, goldenrod
a fever among the sages,
                                        last burning
before the leaves loosen
and let go, before frost sweetens the chokecherries.
The berries still as sour as thirst
this noon.

*

On the path leading down to the creek, I discover
owl's clover, dense spike on a single stalk,
only four corollas awakened into yellow, the others
a sleeping green.
            I kneel down, so close
to that small fire the horizon becomes
the edge of my hand, the view
a dark stem, narrow upsweep of leaves, a few
yellow kernels and the hidden buds
like the many unnamed forms of tenderness.

*

I come out of the hills carrying owl's clover, the so perishable
green floated on the wingspan of the bird whose call
begins at dusk. I ask myself
her question,

who is the beloved:

tickseed, scarlet gaura, scar
on my friend's breast like a pocket for a thumb, *smooth
aster,* my lover in her new dress, denim curve of her hips,
the white of my brother's shirt the night we go dancing, *velvety
goldenrod,* all white shirts
stained beneath the arms by the lambada, *wild
licorice,* the grain of skin on a woman's
collarbone, universal bloom of age, the age
at which your father has died and your mother
is bereft so she must have loved him, *tufted
fleabane, snowberry,* your grief

still mostly wonder, *buffalo berry, blue*
lettuce, but also a numbness in the limbs, *many-flowered*
aster, red clover, white
sweet clover, my lover's mouth as I give her
this last find, which is not an answer, but enough
to close the summer,

                    against the cloud of my hand:
owl's clover.

The Heart As A Way

He weaves through the dry hills, making his own trail in and around grey scrub, slashes of yellow wildflowers, hard grasses clumped along the hillsides. The hills flow around him to the horizon.

His hand strays often to touch the ropy scar over his breastbone, as if he feels a button has come undone. He sees now that the story they told him – how they cut into his heart, how they patched and mended, then closed it up again – is only one way of telling it.

He thinks this place is like his life, lyrical, but haunted by the sense that everything is the same, mile after mile.

All summer he's walked here, early, before the sun becomes a tower of scorched air, driving the heat-adapted prairie creatures into the few trees, or underground. After walking for an hour, he stands at the top of a hill that's different from the others, its far side a vertical cut of exposed clay dropping to the pond at its base. The pond water is thick, the colour of dark lager. A pair of sandpipers step, stiff-legged, around its margins.

How false the mind is, he says to himself, turning back. These hills are nothing like his life. Even the small stones beneath his heels remember, in the flawed gloss of their surfaces, a millennium of ice.

His skin remembers little. He has two scars: a tuck above one eye, and the incision where his ribs were opened to get at his heart. He has never understood the heart as a way of being: *broken, squeezed, stopped, lifted*, people say, casually, of their hearts. But his has been none of these, except the once, and then it shut down completely.

The story the hills have told him is that he's had two hearts. As a young man, it was simple, a pump shaped like his young fist. The second, what's grown in its place since the operation, is a fledgling, a bird beating and beating its new wings.

For the first weeks, he carried it tenderly under his shirt. Now he knows the bird is larger than he imagined. A hawk, say, or an owl.

He'll be leaving soon, returning to his neighbourhood of narrow wooden houses. He's begun to talk to the bird, a little, before he sleeps. To tell it about his home place, where the wren's pure notes rise above the noise of traffic.

He hopes the bird will be content. He has little to offer it, except the promise of the city at night, the back streets like rivers of grey tar among the narrow houses, and the rows of tall windows, incandescent yellow, a forest of leaning, angular moons.

part three

the
GARDEN,
Remembered

Parable Of New Wood

He draws the sheets up over his shoulders, the stale
odour of sickness wafting around him, fainter now
the fever's broken. He must start small, he thinks,
seeing inside his inflamed chest wall
a village, scattered houses and outbuildings
blown apart by storm, streets littered with lightning-struck
trees and downed branches.

He closes his eyes, trying to recall
how the clapboard looked, but sees
only rubble, heaped bricks,
shattered lumber, the mess of exposed wires and leaking
pipes, remains of a wall or roof.
There must be workmen
nearby, he can hear their voices, men pondering
where to begin,
studying the thing from all angles.

He wishes he could lend a hand, but feels sleep
snagging him, pinning his ankles,
his wrists. And then the white wall beside him
has folded over, become the plywood sheet he stands on,
unloading two-by-fours, stacks of slate and shingles.

Where is he exactly, what order
can he make among these warehouse aisles?
He feels good, his muscles loose, his back
strong. He's the nightshift, so he's free
to work at his own pace, alone with all this raw
material. He stops every hour
or two, stepping out for a breath of air,
stretching his arms high above his head, listening.

The men are working on the northern edge
of the village, clearing the debris,
manoeuvring salvaged and fresh boards
into place.
          As he works, sorting nails —
tacks, finishing nails, square-shanked and spacer
nails — he's comforted by sporadic hammering
and shouted questions, by the perfume, along his bare arms,
of new wood.

D-Day

I don't know why I was on the draft for the landing. I was a clerk. Me and another fellow were supposed to distribute food, I guess. Only there was no food. For the landing I'd been reassigned, I was an ordinary rifleman. I was in five boats before I set foot on the beach. First thing, we ran into a mine. But we were lucky, it was the wrong way round, on the pedestal, eh. The boat next to ours – my buddy's – it hit a mine dead on. I saw them go up.

But we were lucky. In their wisdom they decided to back up and we tore a hole in the boat. We were shipping water, a lot of water. You know what happens with those little boats, eh? When one's alongside another and you try to change boats, they jump apart. That was the biggest standing broad jump I've ever made. And then we were in an admiral's boat for a while, cruising around, forty of us. Then they announce over the loudspeaker there's a wounded brigadier on board, they're going back to England. We had to get off, forty of us. And so it went. It took all day.

Strange things happened. One soldier was in the water. He was drowning. A guy jumped in and saved him, despite the waves. You just did things, eh.

By the time we finally hit the beach, I'd lost my rifle. Three of us were separated from the unit. No idea where they were, where anyone was. Spent the night sitting up against a cemetery wall. In the morning, the sea was full of ships, some I'd never seen before. There was a tug with a huge wheel on it. They were laying an oil pipeline!

I went down to the beach to look for my friend, and there he lay. Not a mark on him, not a mark. It was the concussion killed him. It was terrible, that beach. Guys with their heads opened.

I lasted three days. Can't remember eating at all. The only supplies were ammunition. We came across an empty German truck, and that was what saved me. We'd just got into it, five of us, and whatever hit, a mortar maybe, blew the wheels off. I spent the night in a tent with other wounded, a sniper guarding us, an Indian. He had a rifle, a machine gun, some grenades. He told us, "Don't worry, no one's going to get near you." And they didn't.

On the way back to England on the hospital ship it was pretty awful. Guys dying. The nurses had to tend the worst cases. Those of us better off, we just had to stand it best we could. I didn't have a stitch of clothing on, that was the funny thing. They'd cut me out of my uniform. When we landed, I was wearing a green kimona.

A green kimona. I'll never forget that.

Yes

The two men are sitting in webbed lawn chairs on their balcony. The day smells of geraniums, and faintly, of the city below, exhaust from nearby apartment towers, used-up refrigerated air. It is very hot.

The man who has not yet begun to die, though the virus has thinned him to a boyish skeleton, places both hands on the knees of the other man, whose skin is a fungal grey. He moves closer, his head almost touching the other's smooth brow —

Are you tired?

Yes.

Do you want to lie down?

Yes.

Do you want more kisses?

Yes.

They go inside and lie down on the narrow leather divan that a year ago would not have held both of them. They sleep and wake, sleep and wake, until the room darkens and the lights of the city flicker on.

They get up to make supper, though neither of them is hungry or able to eat much. One cuts up the vegetables, puts on rice, while the other stands at the stove, stirring. They sit down with heaped plates.

The lettuce is so green and fragrant in the white bowl, it makes them both smile. They each eat a few mouthfuls, then lean back in their chairs, the apartment quiet except for the hum of an old floor lamp.

They sit on a while, not clearing the dishes away, not looking at one another, the pungency of lemon and garlic like a third presence floating in the air between them.

In This Country

1)
In this country, a writer may die of penury
and loneliness in an apartment in Toronto, her poems
remaindered in bins at Coles and WH Smith,
her death a quiet caesura, in this
country. But in Nigeria, a writer may die with more
ceremony, he is hanged
not once, but five times,
because that government of soldiers and thugs
has a poor grasp of how a gallows
is supposed to work. In Nigeria,

the sun is a god
in eclipse, and this is hard for the people who used to eat
its light, when there was nothing else.
In Nigeria, between the first and last
hanging, Ken Saro-Wiwa sends out last words
to his followers, and he sends them in the red
mouth of the prison guard turned hangman,
who knows, dimly, that the last time his tongue
tasted poetry, he was a boy
writing his first syllables in the dust path leading away
from his village. In Nigeria,

with the noose that would not hold
chafing the cords of blood in his neck, Ken Saro-Wiwa says,
finally, *Take my soul, Lord, but the struggle*
continues.

2)

In this country, no one is hanged. The sun, jocular, full
of itself, pours down on the beggar standing in the wind
at Sherbourne and Bloor, a man who remembers the poet
who gave him oranges, and one day
a mysterious scrap of paper, words on it
he couldn't decipher, his alphabet as narrow
as two street signs. They were lucky
oranges, he could peel them in one
deft push of his thumb, and afterwards his hands
smelled of another country. Just yesterday
he thought he saw her, his poet on a
bicycle, glimpsed her dark head weaving
slowly among the cars. But it was a phantom
rider, hieroglyphic
on his retina. A sign he couldn't read, it left him
still cold, still craving
oranges. In this country, no one

makes speeches on the two hundred ways
to kill the enemy. Although once the beggar's poet
dreamt so much sand
that she learned Arabic and was reborn
a soldier in the desert, learned to love the disciplined
fury of slaughter; had to consume a whole
case of vodka to dream her way home again, obliterate
the taste of burning villages, the sight of the girl
falling between dunes, the secret fear in her throat
spilling. But in this country,

the act of darkness is nothing, no matter
how well executed, she says to me now, her voice
so precise in my right ear, as if she is inventing a new
lexicon, breathing it into me
one red
sibilant at a time. She explains how, in this country
it may be necessary to nail boards over the windows
to shut out the sun, to open up the black
vault of our understanding.
Because in this and any country, she says,
there are no last words
without a little quicksilver
in them, that changeling
light, mother of all
shadows.

The Hypnotist's Wife

He says
      I will sweep you, I will
sleep you into the swing of this
singing hand, wave
before your ticking
eyes
      the watch,
this watch

and you'll loosen, you'll billow
and unclench, slacken into the sling of
the pendulum and the bright
white sheets

          suspending you
above the ground, above the spirited
earth   our snug
bed

         the watch, this
watch   drifts you
breath over
breath   your, my
faint   sweet
cries   you are going, you are
gone under   away from this
mask of sleeplessness that is not
your face   to join
the face beneath
your face   mirror
of stilled water

below your body
lies the body of sleep
                        unlocked
house of my dreaming   your bones
clicking there   softly
knitting
                a shawl, a net, a rocking
hammock

follow me
into the susurrus of mooned sea   the beating
in your skull   be-
calmed   and I
sleep   you
in the cradle of my right hand
in the grave of my mouth

Sleepwalking

1)
Last night's dream waits for him, a perfume
on the pillow. He is walking the beach
breaking shelves of ice with his boots,
the lake he circles not much wider than a pond,
but deep. He wants to walk towards the centre
where ice gives way to water,
but instead lies down on the shore
and sleeps.

Tonight he wonders if he's so tired
he has to sleep even while dreaming.
But what weariness lets him split wood
each morning and then walk the four miles
to his daughter's house and split more for her?
She says she doesn't need it, look at the pile
he's made along her fence. He isn't tired,
but the only wilderness left to him now is sleep.

2)
Sleep is the only wilderness left to him.
He walks the few acres of forest
at the city limits, takes his grandchildren
or goes alone. Enclosed by fields,
it is a woods contained, just as his desire —
to be young again and working
in the north — is contained
by rheumatism and something not quite right
with his blood.

He knows each turn of the path
scored deep between the trees, the stream bed
that fills only in spring, littered with wrappers and cans.
He wants to close his eyes
to the carelessness of others, to understand
that gap at the heart of ice
he paces in sleep, the night inside his head
as he lies awake, galaxy of cold
between the beginning of thought
and its end.

3)
The galaxy that unfolds between its beginning
and its end is a thought that keeps him wakeful.
If everything is streaming away
from everything else, why does he want
to slow it down, to rest
when he has already rested? He guesses
he has at most a year or two
to know what his sleep has earned him.

He lies on his side, hands holding his ankles,
and thinks how small his wife is, her memory
a tiny doll in the basket of his ribs, a stitch
in his side almost a comfort.
During the first years of grief, she flooded his cells
like a drowning, water
in his lungs.

He gets up and slips another slab of birch
into the stove, watches the fire rise and claim
the wood, then bangs the heavy latch closed.
Going to wash soot from his fingers, he reels
under the sudden light, the stars
rushing away. Slumped against the door, he waits
for his breath to catch again, and burn
to ash the last of the standing bones.

The Garden, Remembered

1)
I didn't know then that my time there would be so short.
I stood each morning barefoot among red poppies,
some still opening, tousled but polished
after rain, petals that had already fallen
like wings of blood on the stone path.
I soon hurried away to do who knows what,
turn compost or mend the garden wall.
But the poppies, the poppies I carried
with me, a stain at the base of my pupils, in that pinprick
of darkness, which is the only place I have now
to contain them. I can recall, anytime, their red, closed
after dark and almost black, or in the day, a shuddering
brightness, windblown. Now I am farther from that garden
than I thought possible. Whenever I conjure
the poppies, I can feel the cool wet stones slapping
the just-awakened soles of my feet. I always intended
to take a few seed heads (who, after all,
would miss them?) but it's not surprising, is it,
considering how all that came to an end,
that I never did.

(2)
The day it happened there wasn't much time
but I stood for long minutes in the garden, trying
to learn what I was leaving. I could hear them
thudding and clanging outside the walls,
but inside, where I stood, the stout stems of the lilies
were as they had been, starred with leaves, buds swelling
by the hour, about to unfurl
in their hundreds, the sport called Red Night,
and my favourites, an unknown hybrid,
acid yellow. They were like candelabra, their buds
undifferentiated green flames. I strained to remember,

despite their shouts, nearer now, the master's words
reciting nomenclature, his discourse on new hybrids,
the danger of fundamental change and the virtues
of hybrid vigour. There was no name for this last dazed listing
among the beds, each border just so, neat wooden labels
hidden under leaves, everything in its place and yet no longer
inviolable. Soon their boots would fall here
and here and here. I struggled to touch
and smell and see what I had made, one among
many gardeners, but the last to leave. My mind grasping
at the little of the wilds I knew, seneca root and marsh
hedge-nettle, a recipe the undergardener had given me
for sorrel soup. I had to run, to pack a few provisions,
whatever I could steal from the cellars, and then flee
as the others had done. I stood looking and looking
at a single white iris almost blue against red bricks.
When at last I turned away, tripping over the warm stones
of the courtyard, I walked quickly on the paths, then ran
through raised beds, through long troughs of air
coloured by thyme and tarragon and savory.
But the words that followed me were what lay ahead,
so much unintelligible noise, a language I had never
spoken. That day the garden ceased, the flowers
closed all at once behind me when the garden gate
thumped shut and I raced toward the high trees
and a thousand new names for anguish
and deliverance.

This book is for Doris Wall Larson.

Notes

"Fruitfulness" is for Christopher O'Hagan and Annelise Larson.
"Reply to the Minister of Lilies" is for Patrick Lane.
"Wings" is in memory of the poet Anne Szumigalski.
"Blue" is for my parents, Bill and Jane Philips.
"Yellow" is in memory of Harry Wall.
"Owl's Clover" is for the Sage Hill team, August, 1997, companions in laughter and postmodern baseball: Bonnie, Di, Don, Lee, Rosemary.
"In This Country" was inspired in part by the biography, *Shadow Maker: The Life of Gwendolyn MacEwen*, by Rosemary Sullivan.

Acknowledgments

Earlier versions of some of these poems have appeared in these literary magazines: *arc, Grain, The Malahat Review, Prairie Fire,* and in *Manoa* in the US. "The Clearing" and "Wings" appeared in the Special Canadian issue of *Poetry Wales.* "Learning to Skin" was published in *Fridays After Five: the Feast,* a cookbook/literary anthology (Thistledown Press, 2000).

The author would like to thank the Saskatchewan Arts Board for financial support, the Saskatchewan Writers/Artists' Colony for writing time, and the Sage Hill Writing Experience for the opportunity to teach.

I would also like to thank Lorna Crozier, Doris Wall Larson, and Patrick Lane for their continuing support.

A special thanks to Don McKay for his editorial deftness and his ornithological authority.

Elizabeth Philips won the 1995 Saskatchewan Book Award for Poetry for her collection *Beyond My Keeping*. That book, and her first collection, *Time in a Green Country* (1990), were also published by Coteau. Her work has also appeared in *Western Living*, *The Malahat Review*, *Prairie Fire*, and numerous other publications and anthologies.

Born and raised in Manitoba, Liz Philips is a long time resident of Saskatoon. She is currently the editor in chief of the award-winning literary periodical, *Grain Magazine*.